Body Image Lies Women Believe

And the Truth of Christ That Sets Them Free

Shelley Hitz
with Contributing Authors

Body Image Lies Women Believe
And the Truth of Christ That Sets Them Free

© 2013 Body and Soul Publishing

Published by Body and Soul Publishing
Printed in the United States of America

ISBN-13: 978-0615771403
ISBN-10: 0615771408

Love to read?
Get free Christian books and more at:
www.BodyandSoulPublishing.com/free

Table of Contents

Introduction
Shelley Hitz

Growing up, I was insecure. To outsiders, I looked confident, like I had it "all together." But, on the inside, I was broken and dying a little more each day.

I was really good at hiding my brokenness. You see, no one knew the *real* Shelley as I was ashamed of my true self. I thought that if people knew who I really was on the inside, they would reject me.

As a result, I felt a deep ache - an emptiness. No matter what I did, it would not go away. I tried to fill this void with many things, including the attention of guys. However, if a guy I liked rejected me, the emptiness would return.

I also tried to perfect my looks. And some days I would feel on top of the world because I had a "good hair day." However, if I had a "bad hair day" or received a negative comment about my looks, I would plummet into insecurity again. I rode this rollercoaster of emotions up and down and never found true satisfaction.

The Broken Cup Illustration

Eventually, God gave me an illustration of a "broken cup." I had several tragedies happen in my life including my grandma's murder, an instance of sexual abuse, the loss of two cousins in separate car accidents, my parents' divorce, and the list goes on. These tragedies represented cracks in my cup and brokenness that came into my life. However, instead of bringing my "broken cup," my pain and brokenness, to God for healing, I was trying to deal with it myself.

And so the illustration is this: I was trying to fill my "broken cup" with water from several sources (i.e., guys attention, perfecting my looks, etc.) to fill the emptiness I felt inside. But, no matter what I did, it did not satisfy because my "cup" was not equipped to hold water. The water would simply drain out slowly over time. So, although I might feel temporary satisfaction, it never lasted.

Why?

Well as Oswald Chambers says, "No love of the natural heart is safe unless the human heart has been satisfied by God first."

Having a concern about my physical appearance and wanting to look good is not necessarily wrong in and of itself. However, I learned that trying to satisfy my heart with these things before coming to God became an idol in my life and therefore never satisfied. It was only a temporary fix.

Jeremiah 2:13 says: *"My people have committed two sins; They have forsaken me, the spring of living water and have dug their own cisterns, broken cisterns that cannot hold water."*

I sensed God saying to me, "Shelley, you have committed two sins, you have forsaken Me, the spring of living water and no matter what you do, you will never be satisfied apart from Me. I want you to come to my spring of living water that never runs dry."

God showed me that I was going to other sources of "water" and no matter what I tried, no matter how hard I tried, no matter what I did, my "broken cup" was not capable of holding water. I had to keep going back again and again to these sources as they were only a temporary fix. I am sure some of you have felt the same way before as well.

A Cup That Overflows

I walked through a season in my life when God asked me to surrender my brokenness, my "broken cup" to Him for healing. It was a painful season as I began to face some deep wounds from my past. However, over time, as I surrendered my broken cup to God, He replaced it with His cup - His cup that no longer had any cracks and was able to hold water. As I chose to come to Him each day for His living water, my emptiness was replaced with true satisfaction in Christ.

If you put a mug underneath a waterfall, what will happen? The cup will fill with water and then eventually overflow. And that is what began to happen in my heart. As I was filled with Christ each day, I was not only satisfied in Christ but His

Spirit in me began to overflow. Instead of being needy and going to other people to feel good about myself, I actually had something to give to others. I had love to give. I had joy to give. I had encouragement to share.

Psalm 23:5 says *"My cup overflows..."*

And I love how the amplified version says it, *"My [brimming] cup runs over..."* This is a picture of having more than enough.

Philippians 4:19 (AMP) says, *"And my God will liberally supply (fill to the full) your every need according to His riches in glory in Christ Jesus."*

Do we truly believe that God is going to fill us to the full? More often than I care to admit, I find myself simply scraping by, barely getting through the day. Have you ever felt that way? I still have days where I pray, *"Lord, help me just get through this day."* I start thinking like a minimalist again. However, God is asking me to change my thinking and instead pray, *"Lord, fill me to the full! How do you want to use me today?"*

One of my friends says she prays about the small decisions in her life, like which grocery store she should shop at each week. She prays about it and then waits to hear from God. For example, she will sense that she is to go grocery shopping at Kroger on Tuesday morning. And it is amazing to hear her stories of what happens when she listens and then obeys. She told me one day, "Shelley, I was at the grocery store and ran into someone I knew. We ended up talking and I had the opportunity to pray with her right there in the grocery aisle." She says God opens doors for ministry in even the most mundane tasks of her day simply because she asks Him. How about you? Do you think about asking God for direction in which grocery store to shop at and on which day? When we come to God with a minimalist attitude, trying to just make it through the day and get our needs met, we often miss opportunities like this.

The Chrysalis

"Therefore if anyone is in Christ, he is a new creation. The old has gone, the new has come." 2 Corinthians 5:17

I love the story of the chrysalis: a caterpillar that spends time in a cocoon and finally emerges as a beautiful butterfly. It takes <u>time</u> for the caterpillar to become a butterfly. In fact, if someone would try to speed up the process and cut open the cocoon early, the butterfly would die. It has to go through the entire process in order to emerge as something completely different... and beautiful.

Most of the time, we look for an instant fix in our culture. We look for instant gratification instead of allowing God to take us through the entire process of healing He has for us. Some of us may still be caterpillars; we are still be seeking and searching spiritually. Some of us may be in the cocoon where God is doing a major work and healing in our lives. And then some of us may have emerged from the cocoon as changed... a beautiful butterfly that God is using in powerful ways.

We Are Each Created Unique

God has created each one of us with unique abilities, unique talents and a unique personality. As women we are influencers and God has given us that role and our beauty to share with others. Yet so often we settle for a counterfeit. The enemy has counterfeited our idea of beauty, convincing us to share our beauty with the world in a distorted way. Today that often means that we see our beauty as what we look like on the outside.

John 10:10 says, *"The thief comes only to steal, kill and destroy (your beauty); I (Jesus) have come that (you) may have life, and have it to the full."* (additions mine). I inserted "your beauty" because I believe that the enemy wants to destroy your inner beauty – your uniqueness. But Jesus has come so that you can have life, and have it to the full.

Real Stories of Overcoming Body Image Lies Women Believe with God's Truth

Throughout this book, Christian women share their stories of how they have struggled with body image lies and a distorted view of themselves. However, each of their stories also contains hope – the hope of replacing these lies with God's truth. Our prayer for you is that you find encouragement within these pages and allow Christ to transform you with His truth.

Thank you for joining us on this journey!

Chapter 1: The Oasis of Hope
Janet Perez Eckles

A baby camel asked his mother, "Why do we have such large hoofs on our feet?"

She turned to him. "God made us that way for a very special reason," and she began her explanation. "The big hoofs are to keep us from sinking into the sand."

"Oh! So why do we have long eyelashes?"

"It's to protect our eyes from the sand."

"Why the big humps?"

"That is to store fat and have enough energy to go long distances in the hot desert!"

"I see!" the baby camel stretched his neck and looked up at his mother, "The big hoofs are to keep from sinking into the sand, the long eyelashes are to keep the sand out of our eyes, and the humps are to store energy to travel long distances... then what are we doing in this cage in the middle of a zoo?"

~~*~*

Like the camel, I had asked the same kind of questions. When a retinal disease robbed my eyesight at 31, I initially locked myself in a cage of self-pity and bitterness.

The feelings of worthlessness and misery as a blind mom and wife taunted my sleepless nights.

"Why me?" I often asked. But no answer came. Instead what came at me constantly was images of the new me - a person worthless, unproductive and ugly.

My 3 small sons needed me and I couldn't care for them. My husband depended on me and I couldn't do my part for the house. I dreamed good things for our family and for our future. But what I faced was the nightmare of what I had become.

I paced inside that cage, painfully aware I didn't belong inside those bars. I belonged out there somewhere else. Outside, in the freedom of a life, normal, satisfied, productive, and happy.

And to reach happiness, my needs had to be met. To be fulfilled my plans needed to work out. And to expect a future, I needed my health and that included eyesight.

My face pressed against the bars of the cage of self-pity - I poured my lament before the Lord. But one day, one beautiful day, His Word visited my soul: "*'For I know the plans I have for you', says the Lord, 'plans to prosper you and not to harm you. Plans to give you a hope and a future.'*" (Jeremiah 29:11).

He knew the plans - and those plans were for good things. His design included promises for hope and for a future. I inhaled this truth, pondered on His Words, smiled at the reassurance and wisdom entered my heart.

Reality smiled at me. Heavens! What was I thinking? Those bars were self-imposed. But worst of all, I'd supported them with the cold metal of my negative attitude and incorrect self-image.

Eventually, itching to get out of my cell of discontent, I opened my ears to continue to hear God's reassuring whisper - sight or no sight, He had created me for a purpose, a specific journey and complete freedom.

With His strength filling my soul, I broke down those bars and stepped out into the desert of life. I trudged through the heat with faith, determination and drive. I endured the blistering sun of challenges with perseverance, trust in God and large doses of strength drawn from His promises. I quenched my thirst with fresh inspiration and encouragement. And the hooves of confidence in God kept me from sinking into the sand of insecurity.

Thinking ahead, I made sure I'd stored a healthy supply of wisdom and positive attitude to take me through the long haul.

Goodness gracious. Each time I reached another point in my journey, my eyes saw a whole new world with opportunities to make a difference. To bring vision to those who don't see. To point out possibilities when circumstances seem dark. And best of all, I was delighted with the affirmation that I was indeed created for much more!

Bars come in all sizes. In all shapes. Some are physical, others are emotional or even mental. But none can withstand the power of God, His Word that changes the image of who we are, breaks down strongholds of doubt, sorrow, heartache, and pain.

Holding the key in my hand, I relish in the freedom God brought, the scenery He painted and the oasis of hope in the desert of life.

Body Image Lie: Beauty is something you see.

God's Truth: True beauty comes from the inside and is seen not with the eyes, but with the heart.

Chapter 2: Flawless
Heather Hart

When we think about body image lies, it's easy to look at other people, and point out the lies that they believe. However, it's not always so easy to see the lies that we ourselves believe.

If you were to ask me to define body image lies, I would normally say something like, a body image lie is believing that you have to be a size 3 to be beautiful, or that in order to be truly beautiful, you have to have a perfect complexion. I know that those things aren't true, yet I see girls struggling with them all the time – I have even struggled with them myself even though I know them to be lies. But the lie that I spent most of my life believing was even more deceiving.

You see, I had cancer. Not normal cancer (if there is such a thing), but retinal blastoma – cancerous tumors had formed in my right eye and the only treatment was to remove it. Yes, some very talented specialists made me a prosthetic, but my eye was far from real and as far as I was concerned I would never be beautiful. Real beauty wasn't fake, and I had a fake eye. My face wasn't perfectly symmetrical and therefore I was flawed.

It was the hardest to deal with when I was still in grade school. Each time I met someone new and they asked me about it I would go home and cry. Every time I put on eye shadow for a dance recital it just seemed to highlight my imperfection and I couldn't stand it. You would never believe just how excited I was when we realized that I was allergic to make-up. Even though eye make-up never affected me, I had a solid excuse to avoid it.

Over the years I matured, I learned to accept that I would never be beautiful, and for the most part I didn't let that get to me – but I was still believing the lie. I truly believed that beauty was external, and to me, my beauty (or lack thereof) was portrayed by the flawed face looking back at me in the mirror.

In college I was introduced to the term "Butter Face" (short for 'but her face'). The guys in my class assured me that they weren't using it in reference to me, but once they defined the term, I knew it described me well. It was the perfect term to describe the way that I had felt all of my life, and while other girls went to the gym or to get makeovers to perfect their beauty, I knew that there was no way to "fix" me.

I spent countless hours over the course of my life begging God through prayer to make me whole and miraculously heal my eye – but it never happened. On occasion God would use my deformity (as I saw it) to teach me something or to make me thankful, and eventually I stopped praying to be healed – but I still didn't believe that

I was beautiful. How could I? I could clearly see in the mirror that I was far from perfect, and only perfect people are beautiful... right?

Have you ever read "Song of Songs"? It's this beautiful book that records Christ's feelings towards His church. It's like His personal love letter to us. I avoided it as a child because I thought it was inappropriate as it written from the point of view that Christ is our husband, and we are His beloved bride, but when I finally read it, you will never believe what it said: *"All beautiful you are, my darling; there is no flaw in you."* (4:7) This was Christ's personal love letter to me, and it called me His *flawless* one (5:2).

Flawless!

I still find it hard to believe that I'm flawless sometimes, but God's Word says it, therefore it must be true. And that means that I've been looking at things all wrong. The cancer that I viewed as depriving me of beauty, God didn't see as a flaw. He wasn't in heaven raging mad that my face wasn't perfectly symmetrical, He saw me as flawless.

I knew 1 Peter 3:3-4 inside out, but I had always believed that somehow it didn't apply to me. I thought it was referring just to clothing, hair and make-up, and I didn't struggle with those things. In fact, because I knew that I would never be beautiful on the outside, I thought I had a leg up over everyone else - a head start to understanding beauty.

But I had totally missed the point.

While I knew that true beauty came from the inside, I had missed the fact that God doesn't make mistakes. He makes us who we are – forming us in our mother's wombs (Ps. 139:13), and what we see as our imperfections He sees as His beautiful creation.

It took more years than I care to admit, but I finally saw the lie for what it was, and God's truth set me free.

Body Image Lie: I will never be beautiful because I am not perfect.

God's Truth: I was created flawlessly.

Chapter 3: Letting Others Decide Your Image of Your Body

Monica S.

I am a 38 year old mother of three children - two of which are girls and I am trying to ensure their journey in accepting their body and body image is vastly different than my own experience.

My journey with poor body image began in my teens. I played soccer from youth through college and had an athletic, slender build but along with athletics, I also competed in pageants. Upon winning, or placing, you are often taken backstage where you are given immediate feedback from the judges in order to improve for the next competitive level. I was told such horrifying things about my body and BELIEVED these strangers, as opposed to knowing that I really took care of my body and that their opinions were just that, opinions.

As this was a forum to be judged, that really damaged me for years where these untruths became truths and it turned into cycles of dieting and really beating my body up instead of accepting that this was my build and as long as I ate well and exercised, no one's opinions should count. It wasn't until I was blessed by God with three beautiful children, that I was in AWE of my body and what it is capable of - despite such punishment. Regardless of shape, size, weight measurements I was stunned that my body could carry, sustain and bring forth life.

Sure, I don't have the perfect body and it occasionally does bother me, but overall, I appreciate my body for the work it does in keeping me alive and for bringing forth life. If I could talk to my 15 year old self, I would tell her that her body is a beautiful gift from God. Eat healthy, whole foods, exercise for the pleasure of exercising, and be in love with the thumbprint that is so special, there is not another like it.

Body Image Lie: My body is unacceptable because I allowed someone else's observation to become my truth.

God's Truth: My body is a beautiful machine, perfectly crafted to sustain and bring forth life.

Chapter 4: My Reflection / Her Reflection
Boo-Boo

I grew-up with a very low self-esteem. From the time I was 10 years old, I thought I was an ugly girl; it didn't help that my brother would call me all sorts of names. As I got older I started to get on diets - never happy with the way I looked. At the age of 16 I changed my image (80's look) tease hair and wore short skirts. At 18 I was born again and started to have a relationship with God, but I was still fighting with how I felt about my looks.

God blessed me in 1994 when I married my husband. I thought everything was okay, but by our second year my insecurities over my body image got worse. I didn't even want my husband to touch me. I battled this for many years. In 2000 I became a mom and 2002 I was blessed with my second daughter. A couple of years ago one of my daughters asked me why dad was in almost every picture with them and not me. I don't remember what I told her, but I couldn't tell her the truth: "that mom did not like taking pictures because I thought I was ugly."

That was when God spoke to me.

I realized that if I continued on this path my daughters might follow it. With lots of prayer and learning to accept myself, that God created me and loved me, I no longer hide from the camera and I talk to my girls about how we must love ourselves first - that our inner beauty reflects on the outside.

When people mention, "there is something special about you." I tell them that it is God's love reflecting on the outside. My only regret is that of the missing pictures I never took with my daughters as they were growing up.

<u>Body Image Lie:</u> I am ugly.

<u>God's Truth:</u> My true beauty comes from God's love inside of me, reflecting on the outside.

Chapter 5: God's Truth vs. the Enemies' Lies
Charlotte Ross

I used to be scared of being rejected and alone. I wanted to be wanted. Accepted. Noticed. Desired. I craved to be someone who was loved by all. But knowing myself and the way I thought, the very depths of my own selfish desires, I couldn't see how anyone could love me for who I was. So I always tried to be someone else.

The result of this was a deep-seated need to control my outward appearance. I had to control who I was so that people wouldn't see the real me, because there was no way they could love the real me. This in turn led to a series of psychological conflicts. The more I chose to alter my image, the further I strayed from being myself. The further I moved from being myself, the more confused I became about who I was. Eating disorders, self-harm, unhealthy relationships all became addictions that spiraled out of my control until I was truly lost.

I used lies as a mask to become someone. I lived these lies so that the world would want me. I regularly had thoughts like: "I am such a horrible person, I'll never be good enough," and, "everyone must hate me, as much as I hate myself." Before I knew and experienced the love and grace of God, these thoughts would have resulted in burning or starving myself.

Burning myself released my feelings of disgust, making everything ok for a very brief moment. I could take my frustration out on myself, telling myself everything was always my fault. For that spilt second it would be a relief - a sense that I had paid the price for my inadequacy. If anything ever went wrong or someone said something against me, I knew I could turn to the matches as a comfort. Not knowing anything else, it's a comfort when everything else in your life is out of control. It becomes normality.

As the self-harming became too hard to hide I began to starve myself. I lied to both my family and myself so as not to upset anyone. It was always about covering up what was really happening. I would always blame myself for everything and wanted to please everyone. There were so many layers of lies and deceit, I could no longer see clearly. I could never measure up to the standards of the world. I could not be attractive. The devil began to nail that into my soul. I was empty, confused and lost. I no longer knew who I was. I was numb and incomplete. I was manipulating everything - every person, every situation, every thought, every lie.

After years of believing that what the enemy and the world told me was true, I was introduced to a hope that actually existed, a love that was real and people that accepted me for me. That emptiness I once felt is now filled with a joy that is given through an identity in Christ. When life teaches you you're ugly, you're worthless… God tells you, you are loved, cherished and adored; you are His daughter made in His image. There is hope, healing, new life and love through knowing Christ.

My desert storms: God's truth vs. the enemies' lies.

<u>Lie:</u> I am ugly.

<u>God's Truth:</u> Song of Solomon 4:9 – *"You have stolen my heart, my sister, my bride; you have stolen my heart with one glance of your eyes, with one jewel of your necklace."*

Song of Songs 4:7 – *"You are altogether beautiful my darling, there is no flaw in you."*

<u>Lie:</u> I am unworthy.

<u>God's Truth:</u> God does not give out gifts to the wrong people, he does not make mistakes!

Romans 11:29 MSG – *"God's gifts and God's call are under full warranty—never cancelled, never rescinded."*

<u>Lie:</u> I am a failure.

<u>God's Truth:</u> Romans 3:23-24 – *"…for all have sinned and fall short of the glory of God, and all are justified* *freely by his grace through the redemption that came by Christ Jesus."*

Philippians 4:13 KJV - *"I can do all things through Christ which strengtheneth me."*

Storm: When fear consumes me.

My Rescue: 2 Corinthians 12:9-10 – *"But he said to me, 'My grace is sufficient for you, for my power is made perfect in weakness.' Therefore I will boast all the more gladly about my weaknesses, so that Christ's power may rest on me. 10 That is why, for Christ's sake, I delight in weaknesses, in insults, in hardships, in persecutions, in difficulties. For when I am weak, then I am strong."*

God is now using my weaknesses as my strength.

"The Spirit of the Sovereign Lord is on me, because the Lord has anointed me to proclaim good news to the poor. He has sent me to bind up the brokenhearted, to proclaim freedom for the captives and release from darkness for the prisoners." (Isaiah 61:1). I am now passionate about helping girls and women realize Gods plan for their lives - to come alongside them in various walks of life and love them unconditionally. Without God as my strength and guide, my Father and my Savior, this would not be possible. I am a daughter of the King and so are you.

Chapter 6: Fat Pata
by Toni Watts

When I was young I didn't worry about my weight or about how much I ate. As I got older I had people beginning to call me fat. I remember my grandparents always calling me a "fat pata" (puh-tah) whenever I would go to their house. I remember once my grandpa patted my stomach and said, "Do ya hear that? There must be a huge watermelon in there to make that kind of sound." I was maybe 10 years old at the time, but it still hurt me deep inside.

As a teenager I went on several diets and exercised more often. I lost a few pounds but I never reached a point to where I was satisfied. My stomach was never flat enough or the sides of my lower back weren't toned enough. One day I realized that God doesn't look at me from the outside, He looks at my heart. Also we are all fearfully and wonderfully made. Society tricks us into thinking you have to be a size 2 to be beautiful, but in reality we are all beautiful in God's eyes. He has carefully knitted us together and who's to say that we all aren't beautiful?

Body Image Lie: Our beauty is defined by the size of our pants.

God's Truth: God created us all carefully and beautifully.

Chapter 7: Eve
Ami Samuels

I love the change of seasons, and fall is one of my favorite times of year: football games are in full swing, there is beautiful fall foliage, and the breaking out of sweatshirts and jeans from last year. You go to your closet and pull out the most comfortable pair of denim with full intent that they are going to fit. Wrong! You wrestle with them for a few minutes trying to decide if you could actually breathe or sit down in this familiar material from last year. Some years all it takes is to lose a few pounds, coupled with some exercise and those babies will fit just fine. This year it was going to take a dreaded trip to the mall.

One particular day after a long, tiring, depressing trip to my favorite department store, I had accomplished my goal of buying 3 pairs of jeans. But I had tried on at least 12 pairs in multiple sizes and realized that I had to buy the next size up – ugh! - that is if I wanted to be able to breathe and/or sit down.

As I made my way to my car, I called a friend. As she answered her phone, the conversation went something like this:

"Hello."

"I hate Eve!"

"Who?"

"You know Eve, as in Adam and Eve!"

"Why do you hate Eve?"

"Well, if she hadn't eaten the forbidden fruit we wouldn't know we need clothes! If we didn't have to wear clothes, then I wouldn't have just spent 2 hours torturing myself trying to find clothes that fit!"

Hysterical laughter came from the other end of the line.

Wouldn't it be convenient for me to blame Eve for my poor choices? In reality, it is my lack of discipline and self control that got me in the next size up, not Eve. The lie that I have chosen to believe over the years was that my worth was in a number. Everything would be ok if I was the perfect size or I was the right weight.

The truth is that "I am fearfully and wonderfully made" (Psalm 139:14), and so are you.

I have never read in the Bible that a number on the scale or in the back of your favorite jeans is important to God. I do believe that we are to take care of our bodies by eating healthy and exercising, but not by obsessing over a number.

Body Image Lie: Your value comes from a number associated with your weight.

God's Truth: Your true value comes from God.

Chapter 8: Eyes Wide Open
Juliet Roberto

Tenth Avenue North has a song called "Strong Enough to Save", and in that song is a little line that says: "Fear is just a lie." In a video journal on YouTube, Tenth Ave front man, Mike Donehey, explains this phrase. In a novel called "The Brothers Karamazof," he read this: "Avoid fear, for fear is simply the consequence of every lie." He explains this as meaning: "Fear happens when we believe a lie. Almost every fear in our life can be overcome if we somehow trace that fear back to a lie."

Ever since I was a young girl, I had believed a lie. A lie that caused me many sleepless, tearstained, heartbroken nights. A lie that caused me to hate myself. A lie that consumed me for years. A lie that said, "You are not beautiful." I have been overweight my entire life. For ten years, every morning I would look in the mirror and see an ugly, fat girl. I loved my Savior with all that I was, but I hated myself for all that I wasn't. And because I believed this lie, I was afraid. Every single day, I was afraid of being made fun of at school. I was afraid that I would never have a boyfriend or be skinny or be able to wear the clothes I wanted to. And deep down, I was afraid that I would never, ever be beautiful.

About three months ago, I was curled up on my bed, crying my eyes out because I had had what I call a "fat" day - one of those days where I just felt ugly and I didn't want to be around people or talk to anyone. I had my Tenth Avenue North CD playing (go figure) and the song "Any Other Way" came on. The song is from the P.O.V. of Christ, and towards the end, a certain phrase is repeated over, and over, and over, and it is this: "I won't close my eyes." Think about it - "I won't close my eyes."

In society, beauty is a thin line and while we're busy trying to balance on that line, we forget that to the only One whose opinion truly matters there is only one definition of beauty. He is beautiful. He created "beautiful." He is the epitome of beauty. If anyone should be judging what we look like, it should be Him. In all fairness, when He looks at us, He should turn away in disgust. He is the most beautiful creature ever created, and if I were Him, I wouldn't want to look at me either - but that's just the thing, He does. He sees me, and despite myself, He does not close His eyes. The Bible declares that we were made in His own image, and that's not just the cheerleaders, it's the fat girls, the tall girls, the short girls, the nerds, the girls no guy has ever given a second look. And when He looks at each and every one of us, He does not close His eyes.

I realized that the lie I had believed for so many years was not true, and because of this revelation I realized, also, that I no longer had to be afraid. I had no reason to be afraid of never being beautiful because I knew that Jesus Christ loves me just the way I am, and no number of pounds I could ever lose could ever make Him love me any more or less. Understanding what Jesus Christ sees when He looks at me made me realize that I did not have to be good enough for anyone. I am beautiful to Christ. He loves me just the way I am, and no one - not even myself - will ever convince me otherwise again.

Body Image Lie: You have to be skinny to be beautiful.

God's Truth: God loves us just the way we are.

Chapter 9: God Made Me Free from the Swarming Bees

Jeanette Yates

Although I have been a Christian most of my life, I did not truly develop a relationship with the Lord until 7 years ago. It was at that time that I was asked by my husband and several friends to seek help for what they called my "eating problem". So, at age 30, I reluctantly entered into a recovery program. I say reluctantly, because although I knew I had some eating issues, I did not understand the big deal, I mean don't we all? Every person I know has rules about eating: no fast food, no fried food, no carbs, no meat, no sweets... So what if I just had a few more rules or my rules were stricter than others? And all of my friends worked out 6 times a week, so what if I worked out a little longer, a little harder? After all, my great self-control seemed to be working - I was thin, very thin. And isn't that what we all strive to be; thin?

So I entered into this program and it was then that I was introduced to ED. ED is short for Eating Disorder. The therapists give it a human name so that it makes it easier to distinguish the lies "he" tells you from your own thoughts. I realized that all of the rules I had were ED's rules, not mine at all. I was not in control, ED was. These are some typical things that ED would say: "If you skip breakfast, then all the calories you burn at the gym you can eat at lunch." But then lunch would come and he would say: "If you can get by on just a granola bar and an apple, then you can save all those calories for dinner." Then dinner would come: "Come on now, you've made it this far today, don't screw up your diet, save those calories and fat for a special occasion." But of course there was never a special enough occasion to 'blow my diet'.

Once I was able to identify these rules as the lies that they were and became armed with truth about nutrition, I was able to argue with ED - and that is how I spent most of my time. At first, I would negotiate with ED, "I will eat this egg and cheese sandwich, but then we can go to the gym." Or, "I know that we can't work out today, but I need to eat... I will only eat salad." But as I began to learn more about nutrition, ED and I would argue more: ED would say, "Dessert will make you fat," and I would reply, "it takes 3500 extra calories to gain one pound, this one dessert will not matter." ED would say, "You can only eat what you can burn off at the gym," and I would say, "my body needs 1200 calories a day just to run my organs, I need to eat even if I don't work out today." Back and forth ED and I would go every day from the time I woke up until the time I would fall asleep exhausted from the constant battle to rid myself of ED's voice. It was like a constant swarming of bees around me, I was never able to run from the sound of his buzzing lies in my ears.

I was losing the battle with ED because I was fighting the

wrong fight. In the midst of the loud buzzing of lies, I heard God whisper in my ear, "My child, the battle you are fighting is not one of flesh and blood - you are battling with Satan. This you cannot do alone." Of course! I wasn't fighting a physical battle; I was fighting a spiritual one. And according to God's Word in Ephesians 6, if I was to fight this battle, I needed to "be strong in the Lord and in his mighty power." I needed to "put on the full armor of God" to stand against the devil's evil schemes. Daily, usually hourly, I began to pray to God. I asked Him to send His Holy Spirit to fight for me. I began to memorize scriptures to use as an arsenal against ED's lies. Nutritional truths had only helped me so much, but I was still arguing with ED, Satan still had me in his grasp. But Satan was no match for the Truth of God's word. Satan used ED every day, all day to attack me - to engage me in arguments. There were times when the constant buzzing of ED's lies was so loud, that I would literally cry out to the Lord to save me or yell out scripture... If ED was going to be loud, I could be louder.

When I turned my battle over to God, He proved a formidable ally. He provided me with strength each and every day to fight off the constant swarming of lies around me. Eventually, I didn't hear the lies as much, ED's voice was quieter, a distant hum. Then it was gone.

This is not to say that I never hear the distant swarming coming closer, getting louder, but I am ready, standing firm, equipped with the power of the Holy Spirit. What once was a large, intimidating swarm, has now become like the sound of a pesky fly, and no match for God's mighty armor.

Body Image Lie: Your body tells others who you are, what kind of mother, wife, person you are.

God's Truth: *"Do not consider his appearance or his height, for I have rejected him. The Lord does not look at the things a man looks at. Man looks at outward appearance, but the Lord looks at the heart."* - 1 Samuel 16:7

Chapter 10: Broken but Beautiful
Ashley

My whole life I've been your typical "Church Kid." I'm the type of person that's there every time the doors are open. I "got saved" at VBS one summer, just because I thought I had to. However, I never felt like I had a real relationship with God.

Fast forwarding to more recent times, since the eighth grade I really fell away from my faith, letting a lot of different things take over and consume me. I have a younger brother with Autism, which has taken a huge toll on my family and led to many family issues. I also have struggled with an eating disorder.

I have always been an extremely insecure person. I have been obsessed about weight since I was around 5 years old – and my family definitely didn't help. They would constantly comment on my weight and what I ate. They didn't realize what all of that was doing to me.

It wasn't until the summer before my freshman year of high school that I decided that I absolutely HAD to lose weight. My church friends from middle school used to throw up meals to lose weight, so I decided to give it a try.

It became an obsession.

I would skip meals, lie about being hungry, and make myself throw up. I was even hospitalized from fainting twice in five minutes at band practice. I blamed my fainting on "locking my knees" when it was actually because I hadn't eaten in almost 24 hours, and I'm hypoglycemic.

All I cared about was being skinny. I was constantly fainting and not telling anyone because then they would find out I wasn't eating. I also started having heart problems, and still to this day lose my voice all the time from throwing up so much.

While all that was going on... I met this guy. He was really sweet and funny - and he made me feel like I was worth something. He told me constantly how beautiful I was and how I meant the world to him. I had always had a bad feeling about him, yet I just ignored it. He had a very short temper, and, honestly, he was crazy! I didn't want to leave him though, because I thought I would never meet another guy that liked me.

Towards the end of our relationship, he was actually starting to scare me. He didn't care about me as a person like he used too. He turned into a mean and forceful person, and he crossed lines too many lines - emotionally and physically. He scared me, and I really needed to get away, even though I didn't realize it then.

My life, as I saw it, was falling apart: my family was falling apart, I was falling apart, and my relationship with this guy was falling apart. Everything was in shambles. My life was broken.

People would always tell me how they admired my Christian example - and I hated hearing it because I felt like such a fake. I didn't have a relationship with God, I just knew the Bible stories.

My senior year I went to this youth event at my church called Disciple Now. Before that weekend I prayed and prayed that God would speak to me, and that I could somehow get back on the right track. That weekend ended up changing me. I know I was put in that group for a reason. I learned more from that weekend than I have in my entire life! We had amazing Bible studies that spoke to me, eye opening mission opportunities, and a powerful worship time with a guest speaker talking about how we are all fearfully and wonderfully made.

The last night after our Bible study ended, my best friend was talking about how she somehow heard our weekend theme verse wrong, and memorized the wrong verse. The theme verse was 1 Peter 2:9 and she memorized 1 Peter 3:9 by mistake. She was in tears because that verse spoke to her so well! When she was talking about it, I couldn't help but think to myself, "Why doesn't that ever happen to me?" Well, God sure showed me.

The next night I went to a college service at my church with the guy I was dating. Afterwards I was talking to a friend, and he absolutely lost it in front of everyone. He started jumping up and down and yelling in the parking lot, and practically dragged me away from her into his car to scream at me some more.

I went home with tears running down my face. I ran into my room and randomly pulled out my Bible. I decided to try out a Bible study method we learned at Disciple Now on the theme verse, so I turned to 1 Peter 5:9.

"Be self controlled and alert. Your enemy prowls around like a lion looking for someone to devour. Resist him, standing firm in the faith, because you know your brothers are undergoing the same kind of sufferings. And the God of all grace, who called you to his eternal glory in Christ, after you have suffered awhile, he himself will restore you, and make you strong, firm, and steadfast."

After I read that, I realized it was the wrong verse! It wasn't 1 Peter 2:9! What happened to my friend that I was jealous of, ended up happening to me! For the first time in my life, I felt God's presence and His love absolutely consumed me - I cried pretty much all night.

After all the different things that I would consider "sufferings" He restored me - making me strong, firm, and steadfast. I had always felt like something was missing in my life, and that moment that emptiness disappeared. Since then my life has been drastically different.

My relationship with my family has improved, my relationship with that guy is over (hallelujah), and thanks to God I am free of my eating disorder. I still have days when I slip back into those habits, I'm not perfect. However, my God is. I can do ALL things through Christ who gives me strength.

It has been close to a year since all of that has happened, and it is crazy how different my life is. I graduated high school and have started college. I was able to go on my first mission trip, and share my testimony in front of a congregation of Jamaicans. I got to teach at a kid's camp, and start a job where I get to show God's love to kids every day. I've even been talking with people at church about longer term missions in the future. God is SO good, and SO merciful. He can take anyone's life that appears to be broken, and turn it into something beautiful.

Body Image Lie: You need a guy to make you feel beautiful.

Gods Truth: I am fearfully and wonderfully made.

Chapter 11: A Masterpiece
Rachael Allison

Junior High changed the way I looked at myself. Most of my friends were thin while I still had my baby fat. I didn't feel good about my body image and to make matters worse, it seemed that certain people around me felt like they needed to point out my "supposed" flaw. I heard things like, "you're the chubby one" and my sister was "the skinny one." Those words hurt more than I wanted to admit.

A few months before I turned 17, I became very sick and was finally diagnosed with a genetic autoimmune disorder called Celiac Disease. I was so ill I could hardly eat anything, so naturally I lost a lot of weight. When I was well enough to go places again, I noticed the change in my weight, and, if I'm honest, I was feeling pretty good about my new body. I was fitting into sizes that in my "self-conscious mind" thought only skinny people fit. But, the more places I went, the more comments I got from acquaintances about my weight loss. Things like "Wow! You have lost a lot of weight!" and "You are so skinny now!" were being said to me. I even had someone tell me that my sister and I were both tiny now! I felt like all anyone cared about was my appearance and whether I was thin or not. Having those things said to me, whether it was said with good intentions or not, just confirmed in my mind that I was "fat" before my illness. To top it off, the old feeling of "you are not thin enough" was coming back. In a world where it's pushed and pushed to have a magazine perfect body, I just was not fitting the description.

Psalm 139:14 ESV says: *"I praise you, for I am fearfully and wonderfully made. Wonderful are your works; my soul knows it very well."* That's a hard one to live out! Praise God for all the flaws I think I have? I knew that was going to take a lot of prayer. I'm 19 now, and I still struggle with my body image, but I'm not the same self-conscious girl I was in Junior High. I have become more comfortable with the way I look. Knowing I am a creation of God and that every part of me is the work of His hand can make it hard for me not to be excited! The Creator of Heaven and Earth took the time to design me and He thinks I am a Masterpiece! The more time I spend with my Lord and Savior, Jesus Christ, the more I find my self-worth in Him, and realize that I truly am a masterpiece!

Body Image Lie: In order to be beautiful you have to have a magazine perfect body.

God's Truth: I am a masterpiece!

Chapter 12: The Lies of Satan

An excerpt taken from:
Nothing But Your Truth Will Help Me, God!
Rae Lynn DeAngelis

God has a plan for each of our lives. Unfortunately Satan also has a plan for us. Satan's plan includes keeping us held prisoner by his lies and deception. The world would have us believe that we have no control over such things - that we are just helpless victims. I have come to believe this is yet another one of Satan's lies – a lie to keep us captive even longer.

I am so thankful God has shown me the truth. I have learned that although we may indeed be prisoners, the prison door is often locked from the inside. God is waiting for us to come to Him so He can show us where the key is hidden and set us free.

"Likewise the tongue is a small part of the body, but it makes great boasts. Consider what a great forest is set on fire by a small spark. The tongue is also a fire, a world of evil among the parts of the body. It corrupts the whole person, sets the whole course of his life on fire, and is itself set on fire by hell." (James 3:5-6)

Is this Scripture ever true! Words were the very thing Satan used to draw me into his world of lies and deception. At a very young age, Satan began planting lies in my mind - lies that eventually produced a twenty-five year bondage to an eating disorder called bulimia. It saddens me to think Satan would prey upon such innocence, but he is ruthless and evil. The mind of a child is vulnerable and the enemy of our soul knows it. Growing up, Satan took advantage of certain circumstances in my life and began to bend my mind into believing I could only be loved if I were thin.

One of my earliest childhood memories is from when I was three years old. I had two best friends in the neighborhood in which I grew up. We were very close and did everything together; as a matter of fact, we're still good friends to this day. Believe it or not at this young age I started to think I was fat. I really wasn't overweight at the time, but my friends who were both very tiny and petite were my immediate point of reference, so this was how I began to perceive myself.

As I got a bit older, I really did start to become chubby. Kids can be pretty cruel and their hurtful words and comments really took a toll on my self-esteem. Even people in my family would unknowingly say hurtful things. My grandma would often comment on how fat I was getting. I don't believe she intentionally meant to hurt me. Perhaps she thought I needed some motivation to lose weight. Whatever her reason... the affect was I felt awful about myself.

I remember my dad once telling me that if I lost weight he would buy me a whole new wardrobe. I now realize my dad was only trying to help; but at the time I believed I wasn't acceptable to him as I was. I thought he would love me better if I were thin. I do not blame my dad in any way. He was simply a product of his own upbringing. He came from a family that never had to deal with weight issues, so he had no real understanding of how I felt. Satan took full advantage of the situation, however, and as a result I believed his lie. *I could not be loved as I was. I needed to be thin.*

The age of ten was a pretty traumatic time in my life. First of all I started my menstrual cycle, which made me even more self-conscious about my body. The physical changes I was going through caused me to feel isolated; most kids my age were not anywhere near puberty yet. Not only did I feel fat, but I felt self-conscious as well.

These two things alone were enough to cause my self-esteem to plummet - but there was more. It was at this tender age of ten the most traumatic thing in my life occurred; my grandfather molested me.

This was someone who was supposed to protect me, someone I loved and trusted. I was so confused; how could this have happened?

If there were one day that I could completely clear from my past this would be it. This unfortunate event ripped something away from my inner-soul that I can never get back. Childhood sexual abuse to any extent is devastating and life altering. I was forever changed; and once again Satan was right there with his lies.

I believed it must have been my fault. Besides, everyone loved my grandpa; who would ever believe me? Of course I fell for Satan's lies hook, line and sinker. I was an emotional mess. The sad part is I didn't get to be a child for very long.

I really felt awful about my body now and I tried to lose weight but wasn't very successful. I'm not exactly sure how old I was but one day I overheard my parents talking about a friend's niece who had an eating disorder. It was the first time I had heard about such a thing. My parents said the girl would barely eat and when she did eat, she would make herself throw up. I have to tell you this is how warped my thinking was at that time. I thought, wow, you can do that - eat and then get rid of it?

This marked the beginning of an eating disorder called bulimia, which would hold me captive for close to twenty-five years. I can't tell you how many times I tried to stop, yet my resolve never lasted long. I would always start up again.

I thought I had it all under control, but it literally controlled me. No one knew the lie I was living, and I did everything I could to keep it a secret. I knew that what I was doing was wrong, but my fear of gaining weight was too great. Satan had planted so many lies in my head. I believed I would not be loved if I gained weight. I also believed I would never be able to eat like a normal person. I eventually decided this was just something that I was going to have to live with for the rest of my life.

Now fast forward to my mid-thirties. I thought my life was on the right track. God had brought me to a place where I had grown a lot as a Christian woman. I was very involved at my church, both in service and in studying His Word. I eventually got to a place where I wanted more from my relationship with God, but for some reason I just couldn't get there.

Then God revealed to me why. I still had this huge secret I was carrying around, and God revealed to me through the counsel of His Word that if I wanted to get to the next level with Him, I needed to confront my eating disorder and make some changes in my life.

It's funny how the closer I grow in my relationship with God, it seems the more sin I discover in my life. I guess God reveals our sin when He knows we are strong enough to handle it. Little by little He enlightens us so we can weed the sins from our lives.

The thought of trying to weed this one out terrified me! It had been a part of my everyday life for so long I honestly couldn't comprehend how to do it.

"Since we have these promises, dear friends, let us purify ourselves from everything that contaminates body and

spirit, perfecting holiness out of reverence for God." (2 Corinthians 7:1)

Even though I couldn't see how I would ever be free from bulimia, God knew and He had already laid the groundwork for me. I had no idea where to begin but God's Word reassured me.

"Do not be afraid. Stand firm, and you will see the deliverance the LORD will bring you today." (Exodus 14:13)

I am completely awed by God's grace. He was so patient. I am also amazed that He never gave up on me even though I had given up on myself.

It comforts me to know that, throughout everything I had experienced, God was right there with me. He knew exactly what went wrong and how I had become so broken. He knew how I had arrived at the place where I was and He had compassion on me. God was with me when the hurtful things were said; He was with me when the person I trusted stole my innocence; and He was going to be there to set me free.

I had been in a Bible Study with the same small group women for about two years and I realized if I was going to get better, I needed to tell someone about my problem. It needed to be someone I could trust and someone who would hold me accountable for my actions. I finally confided in one of my closest friends. She then encouraged me to talk with the six women in my bible study group. Eventually I mustered up the courage to seek their help as well.

God placed these seven women in my life (Gods perfect number I might add) to help me get better. They became pillars of strength and encouragement; they were God's audible voice and His loving arms that I so desperately needed.

"So do not fear, for I am with you; do not be dismayed, for I am your God. I will strengthen you and help you; I will uphold you with my righteous right hand." (Isaiah 41:10)

By no coincidence God had my study group in the midst of Beth Moore bible study called *Breaking Free*. During week three of the study, I found the key that would unlock my prison door. It was the story in the Gospel of Mark where a man brings his demon-possessed son to Jesus to be healed.

"Jesus asked the boy's father, "How long has he been like this?" "From childhood, he answered. "It has often thrown him into the fire or water to kill him. But if you can do anything, take pity on us and help us." "If you can?" Jesus said. "Everything is possible for him who believes." Immediately the boy's father exclaimed, "I do believe; help me overcome my unbelief!" (Mark 9:21-24)

Wow! At that moment it hit me. I found the key! I realized that my biggest problem was unbelief. I wasn't sure if God really could heal me. So I began praying every day - God help me overcome my unbelief.

Guess what? He did, and little by little I began trusting Him. Finally I said, all right God, I am going to take you at your Word here and believe that you can heal me.

Of course He was always capable. He was just waiting for me to believe it. Since that day, bulimia has no longer been my burden to carry. I have given it over to God - the only One ever capable of taking it from me.

Body Image Lie: You can only be loved if you are thin.

God's Truth: God loves you more than you can imagine, and with His help, you can overcome any lie.

Chapter 13: Beautiful Rose
Trina Shay

My name is Trina, and I struggled with being fat for a long time. Adults accused me of being overweight. Some adults have even printed out diet plans for me, and each time I thought to myself, 'Why is God letting these people accuse me of all this?' Everywhere I went all I saw was heads turning to look at me. I wanted to run - to get out of this world. I actually came close to killing myself. I even thought of taking my family down with me, but God showed me that what people think of you doesn't even matter.

You're you, and God created you for a reason.

If you think you're in this world for nothing, you're wrong - because God doesn't make ANY mistakes. So if you have the same problem, just remember you are a beautiful rose. No matter what, even if people say you're not or if you don't think you are. I challenge you, the next time you look in the mirror don't look at the person who people say you are - that person will try to get you to think you don't matter, that you're a mistake. But look deep inside of yourself. Look for you, your true beauty. Your true beautiful rose.

Body Image Lie: The way you look is a disgusting mistake.

God's Truth: God doesn't make mistakes, and He created you beautifully.

Chapter 14: Day of Atonement
Priscilla

I am a very blessed. I have a beautiful family, wonderful husband, and was raised by godly parents. Yet somehow my life was still missing something and I felt a life of dissatisfaction and unhappiness. One day my life just fell to the ground and I found myself in a time when I couldn't go on and carry through my life anymore. I had this inflammation in my abdomen and gained at least a minimum of 60lbs over my ideal weight and out of nowhere the sickness would come over me and I would be in so much pain - I couldn't seem to overcome it. I was hospitalized once and refused to go back when all they would ask me to do was fast. So at home that is what I would do when I could feel the pain coming on. I tried everything that I knew, but I was enslaved by this illness. When I finally could not go another day, and I mean not one more day, the Lord knows and is so amazing in His timing. I went to go worship my God and I called out to the Lord with all that I had. I asked the Lord what more could I do? "What else is there to do? Just take my body it is yours."

The Lord spoke to me that day and He told me that I didn't love my brother. WHAT???? I could not understand. Well,

I have a brother that I struggled through the years with. We could never connect even as kids and I didn't always agree with how he lived his life and I basically just kept our relationship at a distance. Well the Lord told me you do not love him the way I want you to love him. I tell you I felt such heaviness on me. Even the next day first thing in the morning my husband told me that he felt like I needed to call my brother. Well I lost it!!! I never did anything to hurt him - HE offended me he has hurt me!!! Why should I call and apologize to him.

Later that evening as I began to pray I knew that I was being rebellious. I told the Lord, "Okay, if you arrange the meeting I will apologize." This is the kind of Father that we serve. That day He healed me I felt healing and His love for me even though I had not done my part yet. He arranged our meeting and I apologized for not loving the way I should of. I tell you that His healing began at that point as well. Amazing I'm still amazed. I have never been sick since and I lost all my weight. Every morning I would wake up and more weight would come off. So this is what I say. Give the Lord your heart and He will take care of the rest. Oh how He loves us! Well by the way the day I was healed was on the Jewish holiday -The Day of Atonement.

Body Image Lie: Humans (mainly myself and doctors) are in control of my beauty.

God's Truth: Beauty is in the hands of God, not men.

54

Chapter 15: God Made Me Just the Way He Wanted Me To Be!
Jill Casassa

I always knew I would eventually have beautiful gray hair like my mother (though I was bound and determined to fight it until much, much later in life). One quick look around my 30 something friends would tell me that it was NOT the norm to have (or show) your gray hair. But I got tired of having to dye my hair every month and on top of that, the chemicals in the dye started to have negative physical effects. So, I really wanted to stop - but I felt like I couldn't.

Some of the thoughts that went through my mind were:

~ People would think that I was a frumpy, old-fashioned mom that wouldn't be "in".
~ People would look down upon me and in a way shun me.
~ I would not be attractive with gray hair.
~ Etc.

But, my husband actually took the opposite stance and strongly encouraged me to let my hair be the way God made it. When I would question why in the world he wanted me to go gray, his response would be: "The more you let who God truly made you to be come out, the greater your beauty is to me."

Every night when I would tuck our kids into bed I'd tell them, "God made you just the way He wanted you to be, and He loves you very much." So, why was I not living freely in this truth myself? I was very traumatized by the decision of what to do and took it before the Lord. In one sweet time of prayer, He gave me a vision - a beautiful, amazingly peace-filled, scene of me with completely natural gray hair.

God truly cares about all of the details of our lives, even whether we should go gray or not. When I asked God to give me a verse for my life, He provided Hosea 10:12 which starts out: "Sow for yourselves righteousness..." Well, a little over a year after giving me that verse, the verse that I had read many times in Proverbs 16: (vs. 31) *"Gray hair is a crown of splendor; it is attained by a righteous life,"* had a whole new meaning to me. It brought His desire for my life full circle. My prayer is that, as my hair continues to grow out in its natural gray state, it will symbolize my righteousness growing as well. And, ironically, as the gray comes out more and more as the months go by, I seem to be getting more genuine compliments on my hair than I ever have before - so, I'm obviously not being shunned.

Body Image Lie: In order to be beautiful you have to look like everyone else your age.

God's Truth: God made you just the way He wanted you to be and the more you let who He made you to be come out, the greater your beauty will be.

Chapter 16: Through the Looking Glass
Carol Round

"When I was a child, I talked like a child, I thought like a child, I reasoned like a child. When I became a man, I put childish ways behind me. Now we see but a poor reflection as in a mirror; then we shall see face to face. Now I know in part; then I shall know fully, even as I am fully known. And now these three remain: faith, hope and love. But the greatest of these is love" 1 Corinthians 13:11-13

When I was a child, I struggled with my self-image and my self-esteem. I didn't like what I saw when I looked in the mirror. I was born with naturally curly hair and raised in a humid climate that often created a halo of frizz on my head.

I now realize that my curly hair is a blessing. However, as a teenager growing up in the 60s, I was very sensitive about my wild mane. My locks earned me the nickname Curly Ann - I hated that name, even if it was bestowed with affection by an uncle. I was very sensitive about my hair.

I coveted sleek, straight tresses that flowed around my head when it was tossed over my shoulder to impress a member of the opposite sex. I wanted hair like Cher and other stars portrayed on the cover of popular magazines.

In the days before hair-straightening tools and salon-style straightening products, girls with curly hair didn't have many options. I remember the first time I convinced my mother to use a chemical straightening product on my hair. Although it tamed my locks for a while, it was only a temporary fix.

Forty years later, I still battle my naturally curly hair. It has a mind of its own. My arsenal of hair care products and equipment rival the Pentagon's store of weapons. However, I've come to accept that it is part of who I am.

God is probably smiling at me as I go to war with my hair each morning. No matter how hard I try to subdue my curls, they eventually return to their natural state; however, my thick, naturally curly hair makes me unique.

Uniqueness is part of God's plan. Before we were born, He chose every detail of our bodies, including our hair. He even knows the very number of hairs on our head (Matt. 10:30).

As my relationship with Him has grown, I have come to realize how much He loves me, just the way I am. I now look in the mirror and see a reflection of His creation instead of an image that society dictates with its multitude of "perfect" models on glamour magazine covers.

When I stepped through the looking glass, I began to acknowledge the person in the mirror. I saw myself through His eyes. What I see is love and acceptance. Because I did not fit in with the world's definition of beauty, I felt unworthy. As I have come to know my Savior, I now understand that my self-worth is rooted in Him—and there is no greater love.

Body Image Lie: I am unworthy if I don't fit the world's current definition of beauty.

God's Truth: My self-worth is rooted in Christ, and Christ alone. I am worthy because of Him.

Chapter 17: Have You Fallen for This One?
Shelley Hitz

I think as females, most of us have struggled with body image lies, especially this one.

<u>Body Image Lie:</u> If I can change something about my body, others will finally accept me and I will be able to accept myself.

It is so easy to base our self worth on our looks and our outer appearance because it is the first thing others see in us.

Plus, there are mirrors (or windows) everywhere that constantly remind us of our appearance.

As I started to work on this area in my life, I realized one day that I was addicted to mirrors. I was always checking my appearance to see if I looked okay. Some days I would feel good about what I saw and thought that my hair and/or outfit was cute. However, there were other days I couldn't wait to get home and hide.

Ever feel this way?

Note: One way to know whether or not you are also addicted to mirrors is to deliberately try to avoid them for a day or two. Like me, you may realize it's more of an obsession, or "addiction", than you realized.

What Would You Change About Your Body?

What if you could change one thing about your body, what would you change?

I know my answer without even thinking about it. I bet most of you already know your answer too.

The thing I've struggled with the most has been my acne and the scars it has left behind.

In high school I had a perfect complexion. I even remember someone commenting that my skin looked like a china doll. Well, that soon ended when I entered college.

I'm not sure exactly what caused it - possibly the combination of bad eating habits and hormones. I thought it would just be a short phase and then be gone. But, here I am, now in my 30's and still struggling with breakouts of acne.

UUUGGGGHHHH!!

I've tried most everything from Mary Kay to ProActiv to Arbonne to supplements and vitamins to hormone creams, etc. Nothing has worked. Plus, I have the scars that the acne has left behind to look at every day in the mirror.

So, how did I cope? To compensate for the acne and try to cover it up, I began wearing a lot of makeup.

One day I felt challenged by God to go out to eat with my husband, CJ, without wearing any makeup. I wasn't sure I understood correctly. Go without any makeup?? Surely not.

So I asked God, "Are you sure you want me to do this?"

You see, I was using makeup as a means of self-protection and to feel better about myself. So to go out without any makeup literally felt like I was leaving the house naked! How embarrassing and devastating!

Well, anyway, I did end up obeying God that night and left without a trace of makeup. After a few minutes, I couldn't stand it any longer, so I asked my husband if he noticed anything different about my appearance.

He looked at me and hesitantly said, "You're wearing a new headband?"

I said, "Yes, I am wearing a new headband, but do you notice anything else about my appearance?"

He said "No, I don't."

How ironic. Here I felt "naked" and self conscious and he didn't even notice!

What I learned from that experiment is that most people don't notice my imperfections nearly as much as I do. I'm much harder on myself.

God's Truth: My value comes from God, my Creator, and not from my appearance and what others think of me.

God is teaching me this truth that my value comes from Him and not from my outward appearance. It is okay to desire beauty - it's a God given desire – but not to base my self esteem on it.

Chapter 18: The Opposite Situation
Alison Buck

I love autumn. It's my favorite season, because it's still warm but not as blazing hot as summer, and because I love the brilliant colors that burst forth from the trees. And, oh, the smell in the air on a crisp day! I love being able to wear short-sleeves during the day and light sweaters in the evening. Give me jeans or lounge pants and I am comfortable.   Autumn is harvest time, too – lots of delicious foods to bring in and eat together with loved ones. On the contrary, it's a season of hiding or of dying. As winter approaches, animals work to get fatter and go into hibernation, plants stop producing and turn brown or become bare, and me, well, I love to pile on the cozy, warm clothes to keep my thin frame insulated. You see, I have the opposite body type and metabolism of about 80% of typical American women.

I am 5'7" and have fluctuated weight between 101 – 118 lbs, not counting when I was pregnant, over the last two decades of my life. When I was in high school, I was the envy of the girls who started piling on the pounds during puberty. Of course, that was until in Health class, when we started talking about eating disorders, and I started getting weird looks or out-right antagonistic comments to try and discern if I had a problem with anorexia or bulimia. Even my grandma, whenever I went to visit her, would give me a worried look, shake her head and say, "You need to eat more. You're too skinny!"

The thing is, I can eat just as much as anyone else, including sweets and junk food, and it doesn't seem to stick. I even have tried lifting weights to build muscle, and it takes just as long for me to gain weight as it does for most people to try and lose a few pounds. It has been frustrating, even a real source of anxiety at times, because I have believed the lies of the Enemy.

Body Image Lie #1: I am at risk and could have serious health issues.

Body Image Lie #2: People don't really like me because they're jealous of me and can't stand to be around me.

Body Image Lie #3: My husband won't want to be intimate with me, for fear of hurting me or simply I'm not appealing to him physically, and ultimately I will never be fulfilled or fulfilling.

The truths that I must constantly remind myself are these:

God's Truth: I am a daughter of the King, made in His image, and He loves me and cares for me.

God's Truth: My value is not determined by how others perceive me, or even how I perceive myself, but how God sees me and how I reflect His nature. _Amen !!!_

God's Truth: I am blessed to have true friends and family who do love me for who I am, not for what I look like. _Amen & Amen_

Many times, I talk to the Lord about my concerns and ask Him to help me stay healthy, but more importantly, I want to become more like Him. I have also talked with my doctor on various occasions –before, during, and after pregnancies, as we both monitored my weight and physical changes. At one time, she had to write a special note to my life insurance company saying I was healthier than most of her patients and should qualify without reserve to be insured, despite my "underweight status." She said that I really do not need to be worried, as long as I feel good, eat healthy, exercise and get good rest. Since I have been able to bear children with no complications, there is no reason for alarm. I am grateful for the wisdom that God gives us as human beings who trust and follow His ways.

As I write this, it is summer, which means bathing suit and sundress season. Most likely, it's not most women's favorite time of the year, unless they've seriously worked hard to fit into that special attire. But when I get dressed, I just chuckle at my thin frame and thank God for who He has created me to be. Then, sometimes, I thank Him that sweater season is just around the corner – not to hide in them, but because I love autumn!

Chapter 19: Don't Judge a Book by its Cover
Laney

I have a small, petite, and "fit" build. Many women would look at me and see that as a blessing and something to be desired; however, in many ways, it has been a curse in my life. You see, I learned early on that my physical appearance was a critical factor to my identity and worth. I received a lot of attention because of it, and was even given recognition as a result. As a senior in high school, I was voted "Most Attractive" AND "Best Physique" by my classmates. I had no problems getting boyfriends and many times felt that the only thing they valued in me was my appearance and what my body could offer them. The affirmation I received from my boyfriends revolved around my appearance—I rarely remember being affirmed for my personality or character. Through all of these life experiences, I embraced a lie that said: "My worth and value is only skin deep." *The Devil Deceived me !*

There is much pain rooted in that lie and it impacted the way I acted, dressed, and felt about myself. I have felt like who I was—deep down, beneath the surface—was not good enough. And, as my body has aged and changed as a result of pregnancies, it has been a challenge to feel good about myself. However, I have discovered the truth about who I am in God's Word. First Peter 3:3-4 tells me that my beauty does not come from my outward appearance, but rather, my inner self. And, Psalm 139:13-14 states that God created my inmost being, which was wonderfully made! I can also claim that I am God's masterpiece, as Ephesians 2:10 tells me.

I have learned that what matters most is what God thinks of me. He sees my heart and He loves me because I am His. I can grasp this concept so much more since becoming a parent. I have such deep love for my children, not because of what they look like or because of their accomplishments or behavior, but rather because they are mine. I am God's child and, as it says in Zephaniah 3:17, He takes great delight in me and rejoices over me with singing!

Body Image Lie: My worth and value is only skin deep.

God's Truth: My worth and value are determined by who God says that I am.

Chapter 20: Broken Spirit / New Hope
Karmilia Cruz

Growing up, I was always pretty naive about things. I believed everything I'd hear, so it was no wonder that I'd believe my family when they'd tell me that I didn't look healthy. The truth was that I always was a picky eater, and I also had a very fast metabolism. According to my family, though, I was always way too fat or way too thin. As if things couldn't get any worse, I was also picked on at school. I wasn't pretty. I didn't have the long, radiant hair that most girls had. I didn't have the beautiful, plum lips, the straight teeth, the beautiful blue or green eyes, or the long lean legs. I was short, either too thin or fat, with wild wavy, somewhat curly hair, crooked teeth, and short legs. I saw no beauty in me.

I lived for many years believing this false fact. Even as I starting to develop my pretty looks I still didn't feel "perfect," because I wasn't what everyone described as "beautiful". No matter how many times I heard how beautiful or stunning I looked, I simply couldn't believe it.

It's when I finally got to know God that I finally realized what true beauty was about. The Bible told me that we are fearfully and wonderfully made - regardless of what others think. In the eyes of God, in other words, I was simply beautiful.

It's still a struggle for me to believe that I am beautiful, no matter what anyone says, but that's when I simply remind myself what God says, and that God NEVER lies.

Body Image Lie: You have to fit a certain mold to be beautiful.

God's Truth: God created all of us to be beautiful.

Chapter 21: Wonderfully and Beautifully Made
Loretta Sances

I am a Hispanic and live in rural Minnesota - a predominantly white region. I have been over weight since about sixth grade. When I was in seventh grade I began to get teased on a daily basis. Other kids told me that I was the color of feces' (in more graphic terms), and many of the kids also started saying that I was fat and would never amount to anything because I am Hispanic. I eventually became depressed and gained twenty pounds over one school year. I felt like people hated me and that I was worthless. What made it worse was that even my family began to say the same things. I was miserable and began to believe all of the words that I now know are lies.

I succumbed to the evil lies of the Devil that I was not good enough to be loved not only by people of the other sex but also by God. I made a terrible decision to make myself "loved" by a guy by sophomore year of high school. I thought that if I did "stuff" with him that he would love me. He said he did, and even acted like it for a while, but as time went on he talked to me less and less and then one day I found out that he was dating one of my friends. One that said she was there for me and told me not to be with him anymore. I felt betrayed. I felt even more unloved than I ever had before.

I began attending a church in a neighboring town my junior year and became friends with many of the other teens in the youth group. I went to a youth conference where I told someone about what had been happening. It was the first person that had ever heard the whole story. I told her everything. I thought that it would have made her not like me I thought that she would tell everybody and then they wouldn't like me either. To my extreme surprise she began sharing with me that she once had a similar problem. I was astonished; she was the pastor's daughter. They're never supposed to have problems; they're supposed to be perfect. She then quoted Psalm 139:14 (ESV) *"I praise you, for I am fearfully and wonderfully made. Wonderful are your works; my soul knows it very well."* We are all made in God's image and are exactly the way God wanted us to be. She also told me Psalm 45:11 (ESV) *"...and the king will desire your beauty. Since he is your lord, bow to him."* God loves us and desires to be close to us. That is all that matters. He's GOD AND HE LOVES US - what other people think and say doesn't matter. As long as I love Jesus and He loves me (which is forever), I am perfectly, okay.

Body Image Lie: What other people say I lack in outer beauty, I must make up in other ways.

God's Truth: God loves me just the way He created me – and that is all that matters.

Chapter 22: I am Beautiful... Hair and All
Raina Faith

I have a condition known as, "Hirsutism." This is where a woman grows hair in areas that most other women do not, and not only that, but it is much darker and thicker than usual. I have dealt with this insecurity since I was a young teenager. In the summer, I wore long sleeves to hide my arms. I never wore my hair pulled back, and I rarely showed much skin if it could be avoided. I felt so different - ugly. I thought I was the only woman in the world with this problem. I would literally cry and refuse to date, because I figured that once a guy realized what was going on with my body, he wouldn't want to be around me.

I did a pretty good job at hiding my problem for a while, but then I realized something. First, it's only hair. Why let something as simple as hair cause me to get depressed? And second, I was created by God. I was made in His image, and He loves me just the way I am!

Body Image Lie: I am ugly, I am nasty, and there is nobody else like me.

God's truth: I am beautiful, and my worth has nothing to do with my appearance.

Chapter 23: A Body Image Testimony
Gwen Ebner

As a child I was very short, skinny and had vivid red hair. During my school years, I was called by many names having to do with my looks: Hey red, red-on-the-head, carrot top, shorty, freckles, skinny Gwenie, bird legs, etc. I hated being a redhead and hated being short. My arms were short, my legs were short, my fingers were short, and my feet were small. Those things created their own problems: it was hard to find long sleeve shirts that were the right arm length for me, difficult to find pants the right length, challenging to find shoes in size 5, and difficult to play the piano with such short fingers! I didn't like the genes I had inherited and the way people seemed to make fun of me.

On top of that, the main way I received affirmation at home was for what "I did." For example, I was praised when I made good grades, when I played the piano or organ well, and when I did my chores well. But criticism often followed even a compliment, which seem to negate the praise that was given. This led to a lifetime of workaholism, busyness, and frantic efforts for getting affirmation by what I did and how I looked. As an adult I encountered health problems – allergies, candida, osteoporosis, constipation, stomach problems; as well as, emotional problems – irritability, fear of rejection, trying to control others, approval seeking, and a lack of serenity and peace. I believed I was not okay if I wasn't perfect or accepted by others.

I tried solving my problems with healthy eating. I was fanatically practicing concepts I found in books on healthy living and self-help methodology, willingly embracing alternative methods of healing, and crazily controlling the things that went into my mouth. At one time I had over a hundred books on health and even went through a period of only eating "raw foods". This type of focus on food then created a new problem – a short bout with anorexia and a seriously low body weight of 84 pounds. The short, skinny redhead had just gotten skinnier!

The final blow was a crisis in my marriage. My world was turned upside down and was shaken to the core. I had no more answers. But luckily this time I began turning to Christ for my strength. I began to spend a lot of time in nature, soaking in the God who made me and who had created the beauty and peace of nature. I began to surrender my issues to God, sit in His presence, bask in His love, and meditate on His Word. God began to change me in ways I could never have changed on my own; that was because God was in control now and not me.

I remember some amazing healing God did during this time: healing the relationship between my dad and I and healing all the many lies that I had believed. One day while in a room alone at a retreat center, I sensed God calling me to accept "me" just the way He had made me. I began to offer my short arms, short height, short fingers, small feet, and even my red hair to Him. I embraced each of these parts of me that I had "disowned" and began to accept them as the way God had made me. It was an amazing healing experience for me that day, and the start of a wonderful new way of seeing things!

Whereas I had believed the lie that I had to "look" a certain way and "perform" in a perfect manner; I now began to believe the truth that I am complete in Christ and defined by who I am in Him, not by how I look or the good things I do. My new openness to God and my desperate need for Him motivated me to spend time with God, read His Word, journal, talk to Him, and listen to Him as He talked to me. What an exciting time of growth it was for me!

I am a different person today - peaceful, God-centered, and balanced. People say they experience me as different. And I have no interest in being overly busy or living out of a frantic life style. And these days, I actually like my red hair and petite body! God is now the priority of my life and what He thinks of me is what matters the most!

Body Image Lie: We have to "look" a certain way and "perform" in a perfect manner to be beautiful.

God's Truth: Our beauty is defined by Christ.

Chapter 24: To Be Made Beautiful
Alison Watson

As an unbeliever, lies about beauty swarmed about me like flies and stuck to me like dirt. Picture Pig-Pen, the Charlie Brown character who is perpetually unclean. He is consistently surrounded by a cloud of dust and dirt. He may become clean briefly, but inevitably the muck and grime are attracted to him. Charles Schultz introduced his character in the 1960's in a strip parodying Lord of the Flies. Pig-Pen announced, "I haven't got a name... people just call me things... real insulting things."

Growing up, I was called things too. Some things were insulting, but most were not. At a young age I was called smart, chatty, feisty, strong-willed, and full of energy. As a child it was things like artistic, dramatic, creative, social, but needy. And as a young woman more words were added like independent, temperamental, perfectionist, skinny, and high-achiever. Over time, these were things made up my identity. Not that any ever resonated as true, but as words are repeated, they have a way of sticking.

The uglier ones like airhead or loner tended to get covered up by the more glamorous like pretty and sweet. The insults were the dust and dirt clinging to my bare skin, but the compliments could be woven into a nice quilt or shawl that could be used as covering. A covering that may or may not be flashy, but at the very least it was clean and tidy. And, unlike poor Pig-Pen, I enjoyed many compliments, so it wasn't difficult to weave a large enough covering to hide what was underneath.

Beauty made up a great deal of my covering, along with athleticism, good grades, and very, very good behavior. I wasn't exactly a prime candidate for someone who could recognize sin in her own life. Not that I didn't understand bitterness, anxiety, anger, frustration... those were the sorts of things that I saw in the mirror at those times when the covering came off - usually, when I was alone. But, once the covering went back on, the insecurities were suppressed, hidden safely from view.

Job says, *"I put on righteousness, and it clothed me: my judgment was as a robe and a diadem,"* (29:14 KJV) In like manner, I put on the robe of my own righteousness. And I was not nearly as 'good' as Job. But if any man thinks that he is good, it is only the grace of God that can reveal to him that his goodness is as nothing. And thankfully, thankfully, that is what God did for me.

As I read through the pages of His book, I learned of the sort of person God can accept, and that which He cannot. He cannot accept a liar. My robe was adorned with much accuracy, but underneath were half-truths, understatements, and blatant lies. He cannot accept an adulterer. My robe boasted that I would never even think of such a thing, only to hide a wayward and wandering heart, which could easily be squandered on a passing fancy. Over the years, my robe had grown more and more ornate while what was underneath continued to grow and spread in the darkness.

Knowing how God saw me was painful. So different than the glistening exterior I so carefully maintained. The feeling that I had truly disappointed Him was heavy on me, but in an instant, a strange relief. Suddenly, unexpectedly, everything that I was supposed to be, wanted to be, longed to be, and had so long strived to be was placed on my shoulders in one swift motion as the robe of my own righteousness was removed its colors now appearing muted, its stitching a bit loose, and its edges tattered. My new robe was perfect, sturdy, snug, and surprisingly light-weight. I worried only that the inside lining, which was the silkiest, purest white, would soon be ruined by my terrible dirtiness. I rolled up a sleeve, only to find soft, smooth skin, almost so clean that it shined.

And so I began to wake up to a reality that seemed so presumptuous, I could hardly stand it. That Christ is my righteousness. When God looks at me, He sees His very own Son. He sees righteousness. He sees the law fulfilled, He sees 33 years of sinless life. All the words used to describe Christ now apply to me: faith, tolerance, security, love, endurance, meekness, enthusiasm, obedience... And what He asked for in return was my unbelief, intolerance, insecurity, fear, pride, disobedience... I gave them to Him and He took them. He didn't deserve them, but He took them. *"To appoint unto them that mourn in Zion, to give unto them beauty for ashes, the oil of joy for mourning, the garment of praise for the spirit of heaviness; that they might be called trees of righteousness, the planting of the LORD, that he might be glorified,"* (Isaiah 61:3 KJV).

Now today, as a believer, the truth has set me free indeed. Beauty is still my covering, but it is a different kind of beauty. Not the kind that I strive to put on, but a perfect, unfading, Christ-like beauty, for it is Christ Himself.

Chapter 25: My Haunting Journey From Fashion to Faith

Jennifer Strickland

When I was a little girl, people used to stop my mother in the street and tell her I should become a model. Tall and lean, long blonde hair, sapphire eyes and unmarred skin - modeling seemed like a natural fit. At the age of eight, I started doing fashion shows, photo shoots and mannequin modeling. At seventeen, my career took off when I signed with Nina Blanchard of Los Angeles and she sent me to Europe.

During the next four years, my life was filled with auditions, TV commercials and photo shoots. While attaining a degree from USC, I modeled all over Europe and Australia, appearing in fashion and beauty magazines, catalogues and campaigns.

So proud of their daughter's success, my parents collected the magazines from the international newsstands and framed them in a huge collage on a wall at home. What they didn't know was that I constantly found myself in dangerous situations abroad - even having to physically defend myself from clients, photographers and people on the street.

I lived with models whose lives were riddled with eating disorders, drug abuse and sexual indiscretions. I dealt with criticism and rejection about my imperfections - and I, too, had begun drinking, smoking and doing drugs.

After college, I signed with two of the most influential modeling agencies in the world, FORD New York and FASHION Milan, and moved to Italy, ready to take Milan by storm and hit the runway. As the new face in town, I immediately began working with elite photographers, clients and designers - including the world-renowned Giorgio Armani. I opened his Giorgio and Emporio shows, showcasing his haute-culture and young women's lines to the world. Armani chose to design the makeup for his 1995 Spring Giorgio Collection on my face, and wanted to hire me for a million dollar print campaign.

Yet, at this pinnacle of my career, this place from which there seemed no bounds to what I could achieve, I found myself strikingly unfulfilled. As I saw how the superficiality and flesh-obsessed world of fashion modeling destroyed the self-image of so many young women, and left even those that achieved success without a clear purpose, I began to have a nagging sense that there had to be more to life than this.

After Armani, my career skyrocketed to a frantic pace - I went from studio to studio, country to country, every day dressing up to be a different person: different face, hair, clothes... until the reflection in the mirror revealed a dim resemblance of my former self. I began wondering who the woman in the mirror really was and what her value in the world could be.

Using drugs to quell the loneliness, starving myself for the shows, and being thousands of miles away from home, all began to catch up with me... and this fast-moving train to fame derailed in a painful crash that seemed to take every dream of my young girl's heart out with its wake.

The beauty that my career depended upon finally betrayed me: dark circles under my eyes, terrible acne, and a frame so thin that one could see all the ribs down my back; my face and body bore the toll of a business that treated me as a piece of plastic that could be painted up, broken apart and discarded at will. When my mother saw me over the holidays, she fearfully tried to feed my anorexic-thin body and I put on a few pounds. But when Armani noticed my waist-line had changed, he outright fired me for the shows.

From there, my career took a downhill slide, and I found myself wandering the streets of Florence, Rome and Siena, searching for the meaning of my life. In towering, majestic churches, I got down on my knees and cried out for love, without any hope or faith that my prayers would be answered.

I finally hit rock bottom while working in Munich - numbed with drugs and alcohol, I considered suicide. Little did I know that God had heard my cries and was right there, ready to pick up the pieces of my shattered life.

I soon met a series of strangers whose sage words changed the direction of my steps. By the beer gardens of Munich, I met a man who was handing out New Testaments; he told me about Christ, who loved me enough to die for me, and who rose again, proving His power over death and over the darkness that had consumed my days. This man and his friends brought me to church, got me an English Bible, and God literally used him to save my life.

During this time, I also met a stranger on the street who boldly told me that I could not sell my beauty, I could not sell my face, but that I needed to turn around and go back the way I came - back home to my family where I belonged.

From nearly killing myself in my cold, empty apartment to climbing the snowy mountains of Germany, discovering a Savior that could give me a new life and the love I so yearned for, I experienced the miracle of being sought out by the Creator of the universe and rescued. In the pages of His Word, I found the true meaning of love and discovered the security that comes from being a child of God.

Over time, the Lord has truly transformed my life from the inside out. I have been extraordinarily blessed with three beautiful children and an incredible husband who encourages me to use my gifts for God's glory. And God has given me a purpose: to share His love with the lost, to tell the stories of my life that display so powerfully the beauty that God sees in the heart of every woman, no matter how broken, disheveled or even perfect she may seem from the outside.

Through prayer and Bible study, I have discovered what it means to be His precious creation, His beloved daughter, His beautiful temple, His shining light, and His chosen ambassador in a lost and hurting world. It all begins with shifting our focus: instead of looking at ourselves through the eyes of men, the pictures in magazines, or the reflection in the mirror, we learn to look at ourselves through the eyes of God.

It is only there, in His sight, that we can see our true reflection as immeasurably valuable and beautiful - the women we have always wanted to be. When we finally see who we are in His eyes, we truly begin to walk the radiant life.

Chapter 26: Picture Perfect
*Katie Marie of the Christian
Pop/R&B group, 3.16*

For as long as I can remember, I have loved to write - it was just something that seeped out of me. As a young girl, I constantly wrote poem after poem. It wasn't until my young adulthood, however, that God took my passion for writing and grew that gift into songwriting.

Over the past 12 years I have written many songs, but BEAUTIFUL is incredibly close to my heart. I will never forget awakening several years ago from a deep sleep to find these lyrics flooding my mind. My brother and I were camped out in Nashville, TN on our producer's floor, working on a new album.

As soon as I awakened, I quickly stumbled in the pitch dark over to a desk where I found pen and paper. Word for word, I scribbled out the lyrics to BEATIFUL. From the moment it was written, I knew it was not just my song, but it was to be an anthem for every woman, young and old.

This song speaks of our true, unique beauty found and created in Christ and God, our Heavenly Creator and Father. No matter how the world sees us or how we even perceive ourselves, the bottom line is: THERE IS ONLY ONE OF EACH OF US! This is a remarkably beautiful truth!

God gave me a saying a few years back to share with you and everyone I meet: "Whoever God made you to be, ROCK WHO YOU ARE!" It is a simple phrase, and yet a very powerful concept.

You may not always like yourself or how you were formed in your mother's womb, but God surely does. He loved and celebrated you so much that He only made one of you to walk this planet. You could search the world from the beginning to the end of time and never find another you.

Instead of picking yourself apart or trying to live up to the ridiculous standards pushed upon you by this temporary world, EMBRACE who you are and exactly how you were made. Amen

The world would not be the same without you - your smile, quirks, beauty marks, sense of humor, and everything else that makes you YOU. The more you accept and celebrate who you are, the easier it will be to stop focusing on insecurities and begin loving others with reckless abandon.

Realize there is only one of you and no one could ever be as good at being you as you! I pray these words resonate deep within your heart for you truly are BEAUTIFUL.

"I praise you because I am fearfully and wonderfully

made; your works are wonderful, I know that full well."
Psalm 139:14

Body Image Lie: What the world sees is what matters.

God's Truth: God loves me just the way He made me –
and that's what matters.

BEAUTIFUL

(You can listen to this song on the 3.16 LIVE website at:
http://www.316live.com/music.html)

Trapped in this world, I can't be myself
If I were invisible would you find just what you're hoping
to see?
Cuz there's so much more
More than you can catch in a glance

I'm giving you the chance to see all of me, all of me
Not just what you wanted to see, but all of me
Strip away every single thought you perceived of me

God made me beautiful like a perfect lullaby
And as I'm rocked to sleep each night He whispers,
"Baby girl, don't cry; there's so much more to you than this
world will ever see...
You and I both know you're the best you there'll ever be"

"Look in my mirror; I'll show you just what I see
Nothing more perfect this side of eternity
So there's no reason for you to turn your face from me

I see your heart; trust me I hear your cries
I'll count each salty tear tonight and put it back in the sky
Call it a shooting star that once rolled down your face
All of those droplets now replaced"

God made me beautiful like a perfect lullaby
And as I'm rocked to sleep each night He whispers,
"Baby girl, don't cry; there's so much more to you than this
world will ever see...
You and I both know you're the best you there'll ever be"

I made you beautiful, I made you beautiful
You're beautiful cuz I made you beautiful
I made you beautiful, I made you beautiful
You're beautiful cuz I made you beautiful

God made me beautiful like a perfect lullaby
And as I'm rocked to sleep each night He whispers,
"Baby girl, don't cry; there's so much more to you than this
world will ever see...
You and I both know you're the best you there'll ever be."

Chapter 27: "Who Am I?"
by Shelley Hitz

I had what I would call an "identity crisis" years ago. I wrote this poem as I began to find my true identity in Christ. I had an encounter with God during a time of worship at a conference, and afterwards God gave me this poem to describe my experience. Maybe you can relate to my struggles to find my true identity:

Who am I?

My first answer would probably be my name. But, my name does not describe who I am on the inside.

I could then give the title of my profession. But that is what I do.

I could then tell you I am a wife, a sister, and a daughter. But those are my relationships.

I ask again...Who am I?

I could describe myself as an extrovert and outgoing. That is my personality.

I am organized in planning events. But that is a gift God has given me.

I could describe my appearance, but that is not who I am either.

So many times I have believed what others say I am. If I receive affirmation, then I feel worthwhile.

However, when I receive criticism, then I feel like a failure. I have chosen to ride the roller coaster of emotions, Instead of believing the truth of what God says about me.

I have tried to work harder to prove that I am worthwhile. Yet every time I mess up or fail, I am reminded that I will never measure up.

I will never be pretty enough or talented enough. I will never be skinny enough or do enough good things of the church. I will never be a good enough wife or sister or daughter.

But, I keep trying harder and harder.

I believe the lie that if I continue to try harder, I will finally be "good" enough.

One day, God gently said to me, "Stop trying so hard to prove yourself to others. Get your worth from Me. I've already given it to you. Remember My grace. It's a free gift and nothing you can achieve by trying harder.

Rest in My grace.

You are working so hard to have a certain position in the eyes of others, to be well-liked and to have popularity. You want to be appreciated for what you do.

But I want you to know that you already have an elevated position.

Because you have a relationship with My Son, Jesus Christ, you are a part of My Kingdom as My daughter and co-heir with Christ. Because you are the daughter of a King, you are given the position of being a princess.

You are my princess, a royal princess.

Remember that an earthly princess is not special because of who she is or what she does; she has status and position because of who her dad is - a king. She has royalty in her blood.

You have royalty in your blood as well.

You are the daughter of a King. And no matter what you do, your status will never change.

I have chosen you and I have a plan for your life.
I will not forget you and will be with you always.
I have engraved you in the palm of My hands.

Rest in the knowledge of who you are in Me.

Nothing else will ever be enough.

You are My daughter and I love you!"

Chapter 28: Steps to Overcoming the Lies with God's Truth

Shelley Hitz

Throughout this book, you have read many lies women believe regarding body image. The Bible says that Satan is a liar and is the father of all lies (John 8:44). So if we are believing lies, those lies are originating from Satan.

The Lies Women Believe

What are some of the lies that women believe about beauty and body image?

One common lie women believe is that we are not good enough. I have believed this lie many times. I compare myself to other women and think, "I'm not as talented as her" or "I'm not as pretty as she is."

I remember attending at a Christian wedding a few years ago. As I sat through the wedding ceremony, I was distracted by all of the pretty girls that were sitting around me. I began thinking, "She has a prettier dress than me," or "She looks nicer than I do." And I sensed God say to me, "Shelley, you are doing it again. You are comparing yourself to others instead of getting your worth from Me."

The Comparison Trap

So often we get caught up in the comparison trap, a game where we always lose. Why? Well, God has shown me that we often compare our weaknesses with someone else's strengths. And it is a losing battle. We are all different and created uniquely. We are not intended to be exactly the same. We are part of the body of Christ and we each have our unique role.

For example, would you want to amputate your foot just because it stinks sometimes? No! It has a role to play and you need your foot in order to walk properly, not to mention the pain of an amputation. Therefore, we need to stop believing the lie that we are not good enough and embrace the truth that we are each created uniquely with specific gifts and abilities. *Amen !!!*

Outer Beauty Reigns

Another lie that we believe as women is that our outer beauty reigns, that our beauty is determined by our outward appearance. Therefore, we often ignore our inner beauty in order to focus on perfecting our outer beauty. Or we swing to the other side of the pendulum and ignore our outer beauty all together. Either extreme is not healthy for us as Christian women.

Important

People Pleasing

Another lie we believe is that if we please certain people, we will be accepted. I have fallen into the trap of people pleasing, even to the point of placing my desire to please people above my desire to please God. We might think that in order to be accepted by others and fit in we need to look a certain way. *Amen !!!*

Practical Steps to Overcoming the Lies with God's Truth

In closing, I want to share some practical steps God has used in my life to help me replace the lies of the enemy with God's truth.

Step #1: Recognize the Lie

In a garden, how do you know which plants are weeds? You learn to recognize the weeds as you become familiar with what they look like; you learn to discern the good fruit bearing plants from the weeds. I like to think of this first step of recognizing the lies of the enemy as weed recognition. You begin to recognize the lies in your mind from the truth.

How do we recognize the lies we believe?

First of all, anything that goes against God's Word, the Bible, is a lie from the enemy as it contradicts what God has already said.

Secondly, I believe that there are three different types of thoughts that can come into our minds.

1.) Our thoughts
2.) Lies from the enemy, Satan
3.) Thoughts inspired by the Holy Spirit

Therefore, we have three different sources for the thoughts in our minds. I want to propose that if our thoughts originate from us, they are going to be more analytical, problem solving or connected. These thought may sound like this:

"1+1=2."
"How am I going to figure this out?"
"How am I going to do this?"

How do we know if our thoughts are lies from Satan? Let's look at how the Bible describes Satan – he is described as a deceiver, accuser and liar. So most of the time, if you have thoughts that are deceiving, accusing or lying, guess where those thoughts are coming from? From the enemy. Thoughts like....

"You're not good enough."
"You just messed it all up."
"You lost your chance."
"You look ugly today."

Where are those thoughts coming from? I do not believe they are coming from us or from God, but from the enemy.

Finally, there are thoughts that are inspired by the Holy Spirit. How does the Bible describe the Holy Spirit? As a Comforter, Counselor and Teacher. Thoughts that are comforting, counseling and teaching are most likely from the Holy Spirit. Therefore, they might sound something like this:

"I am loved."
"It's going to be okay. I am not alone."
"I can trust God with this."

As we become aware of the thoughts entering our mind each day, we can start to recognize the lies from the truth.

Remember the illustration about the weeds? Do you want to allow weeds to have reign in your mind and take over, or do you want to uproot the lies and plant God's truth in their place? It's time to recognize the lies and replace them with God's truth!

Step #2: Take Our Stand in the Spiritual Battle.

As followers of Christ, we have the power to command Satan and his demons to leave in the authority of Jesus name. When we resist the devil, he will flee from us. There is a very real spiritual battle waging and the Bible describes it this way:

"Put on the full armor of God so that you can take your stand against the devil's schemes. For our struggle is not against flesh and blood..."

Did you catch that? Our struggle is <u>not</u> against flesh and blood. Our struggle is not with the people in our lives or even ourselves. It goes much deeper than that...it is a spiritual battle.

"...but against the rulers, against the authorities, against the powers of this dark world and against the spiritual forces of evil in the heavenly realms. Therefore put on the full armor of God, so that when the day of evil comes, you may be able to <u>stand your ground</u>, and after you have done everything, to stand." (Ephesians 6:11-13 emphasis added)

"Submit yourselves, then, to God. <u>Resist</u> the devil, and he <u>will flee</u> from you. Come near to God and he will come near to you." James 4:7-9 (emphasis added)

The Greek word for resist is *anthistēmi*. It means to set one's self against, to withstand, resist, oppose, and is the same word used in Ephesians 6:13 as "to take your stand." (http://www.blueletterbible.org/lang/lexicon/lexicon.cfm?Strongs=G436&t=KJV)

I have pictured "taking my stand" as simply standing still. But that is not what this word means, it means to set oneself against – to withstand, to resist, to oppose – it is an action. So the second step is to command Satan and his demons to leave in the authority of Jesus' name. We can simply say:

"Satan, I command you and your demon of _____ (doubt, fear, insecurity, etc.) to leave in Jesus' name."

It may sound weird to you, but honestly it helps. Coming against these lies in the authority of Jesus we can resist the devil and he will flee from us.

The next two steps are connected so I will list them together below.

Step #3: Uproot the Lie by Confessing Our Sin.

Step #4: Repent Asking for God's Forgiveness.

We uproot the lie by confessing our sin of believing the lie. We can also confess any sin that we acted on because of the lie. So if we are struggling with the sin of jealousy as we compare ourselves to other women we could pray something like this:

"Lord, please forgive me for believing the lie that I am not good enough. I also confess my sin of jealousy to You. Please forgive me and help me to repent – to change and be different."

1 John 1:9 is what I call God's Drano verse. If you have clogs (sins) in your life, you simple need to apply His Drano (forgiveness) to remove those clogs (sins). *"If we confess our sins, he is faithful and just and will forgive us our sins and purify us from all unrighteousness."* And then in Luke 5:32 it says: *"I have not come to call the righteous, but sinners to repentance."*

Step #5: Replace the Lies with God's Truth.

The last step is to invite Jesus to come and the Holy Spirit to fill us with His truth, which is the opposite of the lie. So if we are struggling with jealousy we can pray:

"Jesus I ask you to come and for the Holy Spirit to fill me with contentment. Fill me with Your Spirit and love for myself – for who You have created me to be."

"Then you will know the truth and the truth will set you free." John 8:32

How to Replace the Lies with God's Truth

(adapted from "Biblical Healing and Deliverance" by Chester & Betsy Kylstra, p. 141-142)

1. Write out the lies you are believing in your life. Pray for God's wisdom and ask someone you trust to help you. Write them out on paper or a journal.

2. Choose one of the lies.

3. Confess the sin of believing this lie rather than the truth and living your life according to this lie.

4. When applicable, forgive your parents or family members that have passed down this lie to you. Also, forgive any others that have influenced you to form this lie.

5. Repent, asking for God's forgiveness for living your life based upon this lie.

6. Reject the lie and break its power from your life based on what Jesus did for you by dying on the cross.

7. Plant God's truth into your mind in place of the lie. Use the Bible to find scriptures that relate to the area in which you are struggling and write out this truth.

8. Receive this new truth into your belief system as the replacement for the previously removed lie. (Repeat the above steps until you have gone through the entire list of lies).

9. Pray:

 *That God would bring an end to the effects of this lie in your life.

*For this truth to be planted in your heart.

*That the Word of God already in your heart will be brought to the surface of your mind to use as a weapon against future defeating thoughts. (Ephesians 6)

*For the discipline to meditate on this new truth for at least 30 days.

*That the Holy Spirit would make you sensitive to falling back into old thought patterns and to be able to take captive any such thoughts.

*For new habits to be formed in your mind.

10. Find accountability –have someone you trust hold you accountable.

Examples of Replacing a Lie with the Truth

In the past I have taken the time to not only write out the lie that I believed, but also write out the truth of what God said about that situation from the scriptures. I then write the truth on a notecard and carry it around with me. Sometimes I had to take out the card and re-read it multiple times throughout the day to fight the battle within my mind.

Here are just a few of mine that you can use as examples:

Lie: I should not have to live with unfulfilled longings.

Truth: I will always have unfulfilled longings this side of heaven. The deepest longings of my heart cannot be filled by any created thing. If I will accept them, unfulfilled longings will increase my longing for God and for heaven. (Romans 8:23-25; Ephesians 3:11; Hebrews 11:13-16; Psalm 16:11, 73:25; Deuteronomy 8:3; Psalm 34:8-10, Philippians 3:20, 4:1)

~~*~*

Lie: God is not really enough.

106

Truth: God is enough. If I have Him, I have all I need. (Psalm 23:1, 73:23-26; Colossians 2:9-10)

~~*~*

Lie: When I am alone, I am lonely and rejected by others.

Truth: I can enjoy spending time by myself because my Father is always with me - He will never leave me. I am chosen, treasured and loved by Him. (Matthew 28:20; Deuteronomy 26:18)

~~*~*

Lie: I cannot trust God because He has let me down in the past.

Truth: God is faithful and has my best interests in mind, even when I can't understand His ways. He will help me begin to trust Him again. He wants me to trust Him and I want to trust Him. (Lamentations 3:5-6; Isaiah 55:9; Proverbs 3:5-6; Psalm 91:1-3)

~~*~*

Lie: I am not worthy of love.

Truth: The Father loves me completely, thoroughly and perfectly. There's nothing I can do to add or detract from that love. (Isaiah 54:10)

~~*~*

Lie: I am afraid of what the future holds.

Truth: God has plans for me - to prosper me and not to harm me, to give me a hope and a future. I can trust Him with my future. He is walking before me, preparing the way. (Jeremiah 29:11; Isaiah 43:18-19)

~~*~*

Lie: I am ashamed of and regret my decisions and mistakes of the past. I can't forgive myself for what I have done.

Truth: I am free from condemnation. I am precious and honored in the eyes of my Father. I value God's opinion of me more than my past or what others think of me. My value comes from being the daughter of a King. (Romans 8:1-2; Isaiah 43:4; Romans 8:15-17)

~~*~*

I encourage you to come up with your own. Search the scriptures using tools like www.BibleGateway.com, www.YouVersion.com or www.BlueLetterBible.org to find scriptures that relate to what you are going through. Re-word them into truths that you can carry with you and repeat until they replace the lies you have been believing!

108

Summary

Here is a summary of the steps I outlined above to overcome the lies of the enemy with God's truth.

> **Step#1:** Recognize the lies (i.e., weed recognition). *John 10:10*

> **Step #2:** Take our stand in the spiritual battle. Command Satan and his demons to leave in the authority of Jesus name. When we resist the devil, he will flee from us. *Ephesians 6:10-18, James 4:7*

> **Step #3:** Uproot the lie by confessing our sin of believing the lie (and any other sin we acted on because of the lie). *I John 1:9*

> **Step #4:** Repent asking for God's forgiveness for living our lives based upon the lies. *Luke 5:32*

> **Step #5:** Replace the lies with God's truth. Invite Jesus to come and the Holy Spirit to fill us with His truth (the opposite of the lie). *John 8:32*

The Truth...

The truth is our beauty comes from being able to accept ourselves the way God created us.

God says, "I completely, thoroughly and perfectly love you, accept you, and approve of you. You are mine and I have chosen you. Nothing you can do can add or subtract from your beauty. Rest in the beauty I gave you when I created you. Your beauty captivates Me!"

If this is hard for you to accept right now, it may be because you are believing a lie that you are not beautiful. Or there may be unbelief in your heart. If so, stop right now and pray, "Lord, I do believe! Help me to overcome my unbelief and my doubt so that I can accept that you have created me beautiful. You created me with unique gifts, abilities and talents. Empower me to accept the way You created me."

"The King is <u>enthralled by your beauty</u>; honor Him, for He is your Lord." Psalm 45: 11

The Hebrew word, enthralled, means to desire, to long for, to crave, or to prefer.
(<u>http://www.blueletterbible.org/lang/lexicon/lexicon.cfm?S</u> <u>trongs=H183&t=KJV</u>)

God desires you, He longs for you, He craves a relationship with you, and He prefers you – He chooses YOU.

Will you accept His invitation?

I encourage you to take this journey of a relationship with Jesus Christ. He will empower you to overcome the lies of the enemy with His truth.

And always remember…

Your mirror does not define you! When God measures your worth, He puts a tape measure around your heart and not your waist.

Appendix

What Does the Bible Have to Say About Body Image?

<u>1 Corinthians 6:19-20</u> "Do you not know that your body is a temple of the Holy Spirit, who is in you, whom you have received from God? You are not your own; you were bought at a price. Therefore honor God with your body."

<u>Romans 12:2</u> "Do not conform any longer to the pattern of this world, but be transformed by the renewing of your mind. Then you will be able to test and approve what God's will is–his good, pleasing and perfect will."

<u>1 Samuel 16:7</u> "But the Lord said to Samuel, 'Do not consider his appearance or his height, for I have rejected him. The Lord does not look at the things man looks at. Man looks at the outward appearance, but the Lord looks at the heart.'"

<u>Psalms 139:14-16</u> "I praise you because I am fearfully and wonderfully made; your works are wonderful, I know that full well. My frame was not hidden from you when I was made in the secret place. When I was woven together in the depths of the earth, your eyes saw my unformed body. All the days ordained for me were written in your book before one of them came to be."

Philippians 3:20-21 "But our citizenship is in heaven. And we eagerly await a Savior from there, the Lord Jesus Christ, who, by the power that enables him to bring everything under his control, will transform our lowly bodies so that they will be like his glorious body."

Song of Songs 4:7 "All beautiful you are, my darling; there is no flaw in you."

Contributing Author Bios

Janet Perez Eckles

Although blind, Janet Perez Eckles has been inspiring thousands to see the best in life. Her journey from trials to triumph appear in more than 28 anthologies, and in her own releases including #1 bestselling, *Simply Salsa: Dancing without Fear at God's Fiesta, Judson Press, 2011.* www.janetperezeckles.com

Heather Hart

First and foremost a servant of Christ, Heather Hart is co-author and editor of the "Teen Devotionals... for Girls!" series. She enjoys sharing her faith with others through writing and strives to please Christ in all she does. Heather is happily married to the man of her dreams and lives life as a stay-at-home/work-at-home, mother of four, and housewife. You can connect with her online via her website, www.AuthorsHart.com

Monica S.

Monica is a mother of three young children, Jack, Juliet and Evana. She lives in West Lafayette, IN with her husband Craig.

Charlotte Ross

I am passionate about helping girls and women realize Gods plan for their lives. To come alongside them in various walks of life and love them unconditionally. I am a daughter of the king and so are you.

Jeanette Yates

Jeanette Yates, the founder of CORE ministries, felt the Lord's call to develop this ministry after dealing with her own personal issues with body image and eating disorders. Only after working through recovery with a Scriptural and Spiritual basis, did she receive true healing. Jeanette's speaking topics include Healthy Body Image, Walking in Faith, Restoration and Healing through Christ, and many other topics.

Rachael Allison

I'm Rachael, I am 19 years old. I live in beautiful Montana with my parents and sister. I have a strong desire to share what Jesus has done in my life and that others can have the joy I have in Him.

Rae Lynn DeAngelis

Rae Lynn DeAngelis is an author, speaker and ministry leader. She is passionate to share with others her path to freedom through the truth in God's Word. As Founder and President of *Living in Truth Ministries*, Rae Lynn is committed to helping others find freedom from the lies of this world. *Living in Truth Ministries* is a non-profit organization that offers Christian support to women and teens who are living in bondage to eating disorders and poor body image. Through her own personal experience, Rae Lynn helps others find freedom in Christ. www.livingintruthministries.com

Jill Casassa

I have my dream job as a stay-at-home mom and wife. I have been married to my soul mate for 13 years and we have one son and two daughters.

Carol Round

After retiring from a 30-year teaching career, Carol Round was redirected by God to use her love of words to share His Word with others through a weekly faith-based column she has been writing for more than seven years. She is the author of five books, including three collections of her weekly column, and "Journaling with Jesus: How to Draw Closer to God," and the companion workbook, "The 40-

Day Challenge," available through Amazon.com. Her weekly column, "A Matter of Faith," is also posted each Monday at her blog, www.carolaround.com.

Alison Buck

Alison Buck has been married to Nathan for 14 years, and together they have three beautiful children and a border collie. She serves as a Retreat Director for Churches of God, General Conference and works as an HR Recruiter for The RightThing, an ADP company.

Karmilia Cruz

Ever feel that no matter what anyone says, you are not pretty enough, or "perfect" enough. Ever feel that what others say is much more important than what God says about you? We all do, but the real truth is that we are far more precious that we can ever imagine, regardless of what the media, or specific groups of people say.

Gwen Ebner

Gwen Ebner has worked as a music teacher, music therapist, associate pastor and presently teaches at Winebrenner Theological Seminary in the area of Family and Counseling. She has authored three books, written several short articles, and authored a website called Personal-Growth-For-Me.com as a way to support others on the journey of growth and inner healing. You can learn more about Gwen at her website, www.PersonalGrowthforMe.com.

Alison Watson

Alison is currently a stay-at-home wife and mother who serves the Lord and her family at home in southwest Kansas. Her passion is ministering to girls and young women - first and foremost her daughter.
www.dearmissdinah.blogspot.com

Jennifer Strickland

Jennifer Strickland's life is a testimony to what it means to discover the real meaning of beauty. Jennifer is a wife to her best friend Shane and mother of their three beautiful children. She is also a published author, inspirational speaker, and former professional model. As a model, she appeared in TV commercials for Coca-cola, Mercedes Benz, Oil of O'lay and many more; did fashion campaigns for Jordache and Eddie Bauer; appeared in Vogue, Cosmopolitan, Glamour and Seventeen; and at the height of her career, walked the runway for Giorgio Armani.

Jennifer has a B.A. in broadcast journalism from the USC and a Master's degree in Writing and Literature with a focus in Biblical studies. Since she left the modeling industry, she has founded Jennifer Strickland Ministries, which is devoted to events and resources that restore lasting value in women and girls.

Jen's book, Girl Perfect: Confessions of a Former Runway Model, and its Bible Study companion, the Girl Perfect Study Guide, have been featured on Life Today, the 700 Club, and the Joni show. You can find out more about Jen at her website: www.JenniferStrickland.net

Katie Marie

Katie Marie's life is one of unbridled passion and an unrelenting pursuit of Jesus, Savior of the world. As a singer/songwriter, Worship Leader, Speaker, and Author, she lives to experience God on an intimate level daily, and loves to help others draw closer to His beautiful heart. Traveling widely, she constantly keeps her eyes, ears, and heart wide open to recognize and celebrate the unique ways God is romancing her. The prayer of Katie Marie's life is that through her own Love Walk with Christ, others may become inspired to find their personal journey with Jesus.

Get Free Christian Books

Love getting FREE Christian books online? If so, sign up to get notified of new Christian book promotions and never miss out. Then, grab a cup of coffee and enjoy reading the free Christian books You download.

You will also get our FREE report, *"How to Find Free Christian Books Online"* that shows You 7 places You can get new books...for free!

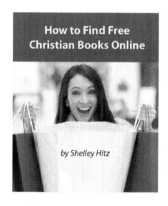

Sign up at:
www.bodyandsoulpublishing.com/freebooks

Happy reading!

CJ and Shelley Hitz

C.J. and Shelley Hitz enjoy sharing God's Truth through their speaking engagements and their writing. On downtime, they enjoy spending time outdoors running, hiking and exploring God's beautiful creation.

To find out more about their ministry or to invite them to your next event, check out their websites at:

www.BodyandSoulPublishing.com
www.ChristianSpeakers.tv

41476072R00073

Made in the USA
San Bernardino, CA
03 July 2019